12147

£4.00

China and the Superpowers

China and the Superpowers

ROY MEDVEDEV

Translated by Harold Shukman

Basil Blackwell

© Roy Medvedev 1986

First published 1986

Basil Blackwell Ltd
108 Cowley Road, Oxford OX4 1JF, UK

Basil Blackwell Inc.
432 Park Avenue South, Suite 1505,
New York, NY 10016, USA

British Library Cataloguing in Publication Data

Medvedev, Roĭ A.
  China and the superpowers.
  1. Soviet Union – Foreign relations – China
  2. China – Foreign relations – Soviet Union
  3. Soviet Union – Foreign relations – 1945–
  4. China – Foreign relations – United States
  5. United States – Foreign relations – China
  6. United States – Foreign relations – 1945–
  I. Title
  327.47051   DK67.7.C6
  ISBN 0-631-13843-9

Library of Congress Cataloging in Publication Data

Medvedev, Roy Aleksandrovich, 1925–
  China and the superpowers.
  1. China – Foreign relations – Soviet Union.
  2. Soviet Union – Foreign relations – China.   3. China –
  Foreign relations – United States.   4. United States –
  Foreign relations – United States.   5. United States –
  Foreign relations – China.   I. Title.
  DS740.5.S65M43 1986   327.51047   85-22337
  ISBN 0-631-13843-9

Typeset by Joshua Associates Limited, Oxford
Printed in Great Britain by
Billing and Sons Ltd, Worcester

Contents

Acknowledgements

The publisher is grateful to the following for permission to reproduce the plates: The BBC Hulton Picture Library for 'Women guerillas on parade' and 'Mao Zedong's fourth wife, Jiang Qing'; Camera Press for 'Soviet troops leaving Port Arthur', 'Khrushchev and Mao Zedong in Peking', 'Mao Zedong as The Rising Sun', 'Cast of the Shanghai–Peking Opera', 'Mao Zedong and President Nixon in 1976' and 'Alexei Kosygin and Zhou Enlai in 1969'; The Photo Source for 'Demonstrators in Peking'; Popperfoto for 'Poster proclaiming friendship', 'Poster showing caricature of the Gang of Four', 'Jiang Gai-shi aboard the USS *Wasp*' and 'Ronald Reagan and Li Xiannian in 1984'; and the Xinhua News Agency for 'Mao Zedong making a report to cadres in 1942', 'Chinese leaving for the Front' and 'Dr Henry Kissinger meets Mao Zedong in 1973'.

Introduction

In the complex world that has evolved since the end of the Second World War, only five states have been declared Great Powers. Two of them, France and China, although they were weak in 1945, were none the less given the power of veto in the United Nations Security Council by courtesy of the three members of the 1945 Yalta Conference, the USA, the USSR and Great Britain. Time, economic development and the logic of the arms race have put Great Britain in the same league as France, their influence no longer global in scope, but more or less limited to Western Europe and some of their former colonies. This has left only three countries as Great Powers, simply by virtue of their being the greatest in military power, in wealth and in population within the groups of nations they lead, one way or another, that is the industrial–capitalist, the industrial–Communist and the developing or Third World nations.

Among the Big Three, each has its own unique advantages: China, the oldest civilization and largest human potential; the Soviet Union the largest territory, richest natural resources and the first successful Communist revolution, which gave it an entirely new kind of political weapon; and the United States the richest and strongest economy in the world, and its democratic traditions. All three were close allies during the Second World War, and though the alliance survived the war, it has not survived the peace. Their interrelations – always as changeable and complex as the interactions of three planets in space, moving in relation to one another under the influence of mutual attraction and mutual repulsion alike – are similarly closely related to the internal developments of each of them.

The history of Russo-Chinese relations – contradictory and complicated – go back hundreds of years. Those between the

United States and China are also more than a hundred years old, and from studying both, we can see how illogical and artificial the Sino-Soviet conflict was during its sharpest phase in the 1960s, when mutual threats and confrontation were the order of the day, and how naïve and illusory was America's intention to try 'to play the China card' in order to advance American foreign policy, as well as America's attempts to use China as a surrogate or even substitute for American power in the Far East and Pacific.

Countries with global ambitions usually either have or have to create a chief adversary. The Soviet Union's global ambitions have mainly been ideological, while those of the United States are chiefly economic. The global ambitions of the Chinese People's Republic were closely connected with Maoism, which managed to thrive with *two* chief adversaries, one being Soviet 'revisionism', the other the imperialist policies of the United States. With the death of Maoism and the end of the global ambitions of China's brand of Communism, it was only natural that regional interests would render unnecessary China's desire to see the United States as a real adversary. Similarly, Chinese antagonism towards the Soviet Union has lost its ideological and political point, and only conflicts of a local character, such as Afghanistan and Kampuchea, remain as serious obstacles to the normalization of Sino-Soviet relations.

I do not believe that the United States policy which sees China as a counterweight to the Soviet Union shows a correct understanding of the Sino-Soviet conflict. Soviet policy towards China has similarly often been wrong and sometimes very dangerous. At the same time, the Chinese perception of both the Soviet Union and the United States, especially during the Maoist era, was false and did great damage to the economic and political development of China itself. Both the United States and the Soviet Union now want to help China, but for different and selfish reasons. The development of a strong China, however, is important for the rest of the world and for world peace only if this great country becomes more independent and more neutral. It is important as a potential counterweight to the two military superpowers.

There is a great amount of literature on the Sino-Soviet conflict at its different stages. This book is not intended as a comprehensive review or complete analysis of the subject, but is rather an attempt to discover a pattern in the complex picture of the past, and to trace possible tendencies for the future. My own interest in China goes back many years. On graduating from Leningrad University in 1950–2, I chose for my postgraduate thesis to analyse the history and characteristics of the Chinese revolution which, both in the forms it took and the nature of its driving forces, was so very different from the Russian revolution. My thesis adviser was Professor G. V. Yefimov, the noted sinologist and Dean of the Oriental Studies Faculty of Leningrad University. I kept up my interest in China, and in subsequent years closely followed both events there and everything that was published on China in the Soviet Union, and at times I also followed what was being said about Sino-Soviet relations in the Western press.

There are many highly expert sinologists in the Soviet Union, and yet everything published here in the past 25 years on recent Chinese history or Sino-Soviet relations, as well as Sino-American relations, is stamped with tendentiousness and constitutes propaganda rather than academic research. Given the continuation of militant Chinese anti-Soviet agitation, it is hard for the time being to expect anything objective on Sino-Soviet relations to come out of China. Nor have Western China specialists succeeding in filling the gap satisfactorily. The German and American books on contemporary China that I have managed to get hold of contain interesting and important material, but they, too, are regrettably not free of tendentiousness, especially when they deal with Sino-Soviet relations, and the main theme of many of them is the notorious 'China card'.

These circumstances have prompted me to try to draw together the results of my own reflections, my observations and the analysis that I have devoted to the subject for many years. I have tried as far as possible to be objective, and to avoid any propaganda clichés. To be sure, a Soviet historian who is an independent researcher to boot is invariably bound to suffer from a lack of sources and materials. Moreover, for an author living in Moscow, it is not easy to write a book on international problems. Many of the Western and Chinese sources that I have used in this book are not currently available in the Soviet Union, and I would therefore like to express my gratitude to my brother, Zhores, now living in London, and to many of my Western friends who, knowing that I intended to write on the subject, have supplied me for many years with books and papers published in the West, and with Western translations of Chinese publications. I am also grateful for the help I have received from friends here in Moscow who helped me by translating from French and Chinese. I am myself responsible for the translation of the German sources that I have used in my research.

Finally, I would be very grateful for any critical comments from my readers, as well as any offprints, clippings and other materials which might indicate errors in my judgement, and which would bring my knowledge of the problem up to date. When one lives in a country where the official policy of the government is both to limit and to shape in a particular way the information available to the general public and the academic community alike, all the help one can get from foreign colleagues is invaluable.

Nearly all the events I have here described took place before my eyes. Many of them I felt deeply, and I related to them not only as a historian, but as an interested witness. I have written my book with a feeling of immutable respect for China and for the great Chinese nation, and for the American nation, but also with a feeling of love for my own country and its people. I feel a deep sense of hope and a desire for the peoples of the Soviet Union, the United States and China to share a future of peace and benevolent co-operation, despite all the differences, which regrettably – or maybe for the good of all mankind – will separate our countries and our peoples for a very long time.

Roy A. Medvedev
Moscow May 1985

1

The USSR and China:
relevant historical events

*The Soviet Union and the national-democratic
revolution in China*

As early as 1911, countless armed mass actions in various
regions of China had led to the successful Wuchang uprising,
from which ensued the Shanghai revolution under the leadership of Sun Yat-sen. Despite the overthrow of the Manchu
Imperial dynasty which followed, Sun Yat-sen was compelled to
decline power as the first president of the Republic of China.
Even so, the revolutionary struggle continued with varied
success, led by the army of the Kuomintang which Sun Yat-sen
had created. By 1917, the influence of this party was limited to
only a few regions of Southern China, chiefly in the province of
Canton (Guangdong). On 25 August 1917 in the capital city of
Canton (Guangzhou) the decision was taken to create a Military
Government of Southern China to be led by Sun Yat-sen. In the
rest of China, the warlords were locked in fierce struggle to
capture the capital of the country in the hope of securing for
themselves recognition as the central government.

While the 1917 October Revolution was taking place in
Russia, the Anhwei group of warlords, led by Duan Qirui, held
power in Peking and the northern provinces of China. This
government, which declared war on Germany, and was recognized by virtually all capitalist countries as the 'legal' government of the whole of China, refused to conduct any talks
whatsoever with the government of Soviet Russia, and after the
onset of the Intervention by the Western powers and Japan, it
sent small detachments of Chinese troops into Siberian territory
and the Far East with the main object of giving support to the
Japanese.

The Civil War in Russia, however, resulted in the defeat of the White armies and the Interventionists. In the summer of 1919, the Red Army began a major offensive against the forces of Admiral Kolchak, 'Supreme Ruler of Siberia', and all his allies. The Soviet government published its famous declaration of 25 July 1919, addressed 'To the Chinese people and the governments of Southern and Northern China', in which the RSFSR repudiated all the unequal treaties and privileges by which tsarist Russia had bound China, and it offered to begin talks with a view to working out a new treaty, based on the recognition of China's full equality and independence. This important document declared:

> After two years of war and unbelievable effort, Soviet Russia and the Red Army are crossing the Urals to the East not in order to do violence, not in order to enslave anyone, and not in search of victories. ... We bring freedom from the yoke of the foreign bayonet and foreign gold which together have been stifling the enslaved peoples of the East, first and foremost among them the people of China. We bring help not only to our own toiling masses, but also to the Chinese people, and we repeat once more what we said to the Chinese people at the time of the Great October Revolution of 1917, and what no doubt the venal American–European–Japanese press kept from them.

The government of the RSFSR announced its repudiation of the indemnities imposed upon China at the time of the Boxer Rebellion of 1900, as well as all agreements with Japan which concerned China and which had been concluded between 1907 and 1916. It expressed readiness to enter talks with China over the cancellation of the 1896 treaty and the Peking Protocol of 1901. The declaration went on: 'The Soviet government repudiates all the conquests by the tsarist regime which seized Manchuria and other provinces from China. Let the nations inhabiting those areas decide for themselves within which state borders they wish to live.'[1]

The Chinese government in Peking did not respond to the declaration, but the first diplomatic contacts between the RSFSR and China were established after the defeat of Kolchak, and even trade relations were renewed, albeit on a very modest scale.[2]

Relations of a more intensive nature were carried on between the RSFSR – renamed the USSR in 1923 – and Sun Yat-sen's revolutionary government of South China, where there was for a time a group of Soviet diplomats, led by A. A. Yoffe, while a military delegation from Sun Yat-sen, under the leadership of Jiang Gai-shi (Chiang Kai-shek), was sent to Moscow. In 1923 the Soviet government provided financial aid to the government of Sun Yat-sen and despatched a team of military and political advisers to South China, led by M. M. Borodin, P. A. Pavlov and B. K. Blyukher. The reorganization of the Kuomintang and the revolutionary Chinese army was carried out by these military and political advisers, and a special military academy was established at Whampoa. Meanwhile, numerous military personnel from the Kuomintang and the Chinese Communist Party – which had been formed in 1921 – were undergoing training in Soviet military academies and schools. At various times, Lin Biao, Deng Xiaoping, Wang Ming and others all studied in Moscow. Jiang Gai-shi, who had been through Japanese military school, spent several months in the USSR studying Red Army war experience. The Chinese Communist Party (CCP) formed a political and military union with the Kuomintang, which at that time was considered to be the most influential revolutionary party in China, while Jiang Gai-shi was regarded as Sun Yat-sen's closest deputy and successor.

By the autumn of 1924, the complicated conflicts among the warlords of northern China had resulted in the growth of influence and power of the nationalist generals who, wishing to exploit Sun Yat-sen's popularity to their own advantage, invited him to visit Peking and take part in a proposed national conference on the country's military and political problems. Sun Yat-sen set sail from Guangzhou (Canton) to Shanghai in November 1924 accompanied by both his own Chinese as well as a number of Soviet advisers. Among the convoy escorting the party out of the harbour was the Soviet warship *Vorovsky*. The trip had enormous propaganda value, but unfortunately Sun Yat-sen, already seriously ill, was unable to return to Guangzhou, and died in Peking on 12 March 1925. The day before he died, and in the presence of the party leaders, he signed two political documents, one his 'Testament to the Kuomintang' and the other a 'Message to the Soviet Union', which read:

Dear Comrades! In parting from you, I want to express my ardent hope that the dawn will soon break. The time will come when the Soviet Union, as a good friend and ally, will welcome a powerful and free China, when in the great struggle for the freedom of the downtrodden nations of the world, both countries will go forward hand in hand and achieve victory.[3]

The history of relations between the Soviet Union and China, however, turned out to be much more complex and dramatic. The new dawn for which Sun Yat-sen had hoped came only a quarter of a century later, and soon the sky above our two countries was once again darkened by clouds of misunderstanding and hostility.

I do not propose to discuss here the events which took place in China in 1925–7: they were merely the initial phase of the national-democratic revolution. The problems connected with those events were under constant discussion, both in Comintern and within the Communist Party of the Soviet Union – at that time still called the All-Russian Communist Party (Bolsheviks) – indeed, the issues of the internal forces and policies of the Chinese revolution became the cause of a fierce factional struggle within the Chinese Communist Party itself, as well as within the Russian Communist Party and Comintern. The revolution brought the Kuomintang (KMT) to power in China, partly thanks to the revolutionary armies' victories over the warlords of the North, but also partly thanks to the compromise made by the most powerful of the warlords with the new leaders of the KMT who had destroyed the union with the Chinese Communist Party and unleashed mass terror against its members.

Diplomatic relations were established between the Soviet Union and China with the signing in Peking on 31 May 1924 of an 'Agreement on general principles for regularizing issues between the Union of Soviet Socialist Republics and the Republic of China'. The new Chinese government, headed by Jiang Gaishi and based by its own choice in the city of Nanjing, conducted an anti-Soviet policy and had to contend with an equally hostile attitude on the part of the Soviet Union. Matters went as far as a short but sharp armed skirmish between the two sides over the seizure of the Chinese Eastern Railway by Chinese troops. The Chinese forces were defeated by the Special Far Eastern Red

Army under the command of B. K. Blyukher, former adviser to the KMT. The matter was settled with the signing of an agreement at Khabarovsk on 29 December 1929, according to which the question of the railway was restored to the previous position. Diplomatic relations with the central KMT government were, however, broken off and were not restored until 1932.

After the treachery of the KMT, the Chinese Communist Party tried to carry on under the old slogans, but it suffered a number of painful defeats in the largest cities of South China. The CCP in particular took upon itself the role of sole leadership of the revolutionary movement of the peasants, workers and lower middle classes. But a new strategy and tactics of revolutionary struggle needed to be worked out.

The discussions over past events as well as the outlook for the Chinese revolution had given rise to a series of conflicts between Soviet and Chinese Communist leaders even before the end of the 1920s. The Soviet party was the dominant force in Comintern and Stalin regarded himself as entitled to interfere in all important matters affecting other communist parties, including even the selection of their leading cadres. The heightened factional struggle within the CCP only facilitated this interference. Events in China, however, were moving along a different path from that imagined by both many Soviet and many Chinese leaders.

It was precisely at the time when the revolutionary movement in the big cities went into decline that a mass revolutionary movement in the remote countryside began to grow. Mao Zedong (Mao Tse-tung) was not the only Chinese Communist leader who recognized the highly important role to be played in the revolution by an armed peasant movement. The most prominent organizer and theoretician of the peasant movement in China was Peng Pai, a member of the Central Committee of the CCP who died in a KMT prison in 1929. Peng Dehuai, He Long and Zhang Guotao all became organizers of Communist power bases in the villages. An authentic, new 'alternative' party leadership began forming in the remote countryside with the group led by Mao Zedong and Zhou Enlai (Chou En-lai) playing the most important role.

The main centres of the CCP at the end of the 1920s were located in Moscow, where in 1928 the party's Sixth Congress took place, and in Shang-hai. Mao's plans to transfer the centre of the revolutionary struggle in China from the large cities to remote rural districts were viewed with reservation, not to say outright hostility, by many Soviet and Comintern leaders. And as the influence of Mao Zedong's group increased, so the ability of Moscow and Comintern to exercise influence over the formation of CCP policy diminished. Nevertheless, Moscow had to face facts. The remarkable successes of the Soviet movement in the rural districts, the formation there of a peasant Red Army, the proliferation of revolutionary support bases, and then the formation of the Central Workers' and Peasants' Government, all brought about a change in Comintern's attitude to the partisan movement of the Chinese peasantry. At the beginning of the 1930s, the journal *Communist International* carried a number of articles praising the successes of the Soviet regions in China, the chairman of the Workers' and Peasants' Government, Mao Zedong, as well as the commander of the Red Army, Zhu De. In due course, Comintern recommended that the CCP's governing institutions be transferred from the underground in Shanghai to one of the support regions of Soviet China.

The period 1931 to 1937 was a time of extraordinarily complicated military and political struggle between, on the one hand, the CCP and the Chinese Red Army, and, on the other, the troops of the KMT and groupings of local warlords. It was a time of victories and defeats, of the Long March and the continuing factional struggle within the leadership of the CCP. In the final outcome, it was Mao Zedong and his closest comrades-in-arms who concentrated the leadership of both party and army in their hands.

An extremely contradictory picture of the factional struggle in the CCP, as well as of the attitude of the Soviet Communist Party and Comintern towards the various factions of the Chinese leadership, emerges from the sources, whether from Soviet accounts published at different times, or Chinese official publications, memoirs of *émigrés*, such as the former CCP Politburo members Zhang Guotao and Wang Ming, or the books and memoirs of foreign participants in the events, for example Otto Braun,[4] or the research of Western sinologists and specialists on the history of Communism. Soviet books and articles published in the 1970s contain a great deal of criticism of Mao Zedong, who is accused of every kind of error and even criminality.[5] It is impossible to judge the validity of these accusations, especially as so many of these publications display a blatant political bias. What is beyond doubt, however, is that the victory of Mao Zedong and his group was due to something more than ambition, cunning and craftiness. Undeniably, it was precisely Mao Zedong who during those years was able to formulate the strategic aims that best conformed to the new phase of the Chinese revolution, aims that made it possible for the CCP and its armed forces to gain several important victories over the armies of the KMT, and that gave Mao Zedong authority as the most powerful political and military strategist, with the greater part of his political capital in the party guaranteed.

After decades of internal wars, in 1937 the Chinese people found themselves faced by new ordeals. Having earlier occupied Manchuria, the Japanese now launched a broad offensive against other regions of China. The Japanese army defeated the KMT troops and took Peking, Tianjin, Nanjing, Zhangjiaokou, Baoding and, by the end of the year, Shanghai. Japan had set out rapidly to subjugate the whole of China and to install a pro-Japanese puppet government. The KMT was compelled to offer armed resistance, and all over the country mobilization began in order to raise an anti-Japanese patriotic movement and repel Japanese aggression.

By 1937 the Chinese Communist Party still controlled only a few spacious, but sparsely populated, regions in the north-west of the country. The size of both the party and the Red Army had been severely diminished, and it was very difficult to maintain contact with the underground organizations in the cities. The war with Japan, however, decisively altered the internal political circumstances in the country. The KMT could not now decline the CCP's offer to co-operate. Jiang Gai-shi had to recognize the legality of the CCP and the Red Army, whose main forces were now renamed the Eighth National-Revolutionary Army. In the autumn of 1937, the central executive committee of the KMT published a manifesto on collaboration between the KMT and the CCP, and the Soviet Union welcomed the announcement.

Counting on a speedy victory in China, Japan had prepared herself for the capture of many other countries in Asia and also for an attack on the Soviet Union, and Japanese troops began to concentrate systematically along the Soviet border. Serious clashes between Soviet and Japanese forces in the Far East occurred in 1937 in the region of Lake Hasan and two years later on Mongolian territory in the region of the River Khalkin Gol. Naturally, the Soviet Union looked to China as an ally. To help the KMT army command, the Soviet Union sent a team of military advisers, and units of the Soviet Air Force were despatched to various fronts in China.[6] The Soviet Union also provided a certain amount of help to the Eighth Army and to the Special Zone which was the chief support base of the CCP. Apart from a number of doctors, some political representatives were also sent to the Special Zone and served there chiefly as observers. But under the circumstances, this help was barely significant.

During the years of the war with Japan, the Chinese Communists slowly but surely strengthened their positions and increased their influence in the country. It was precisely under the leadership of the CCP that the partisan movement developed in the regions under Japanese occupation. New support bases were created there and new armed forces which were soon combined to form the Fourth National Revolutionary Army. All this increased friction between the Chinese central government, now located in Chongqing under Jiang Gai-shi, and the CCP. A sudden assault by the KMT on the Fourth Army's headquarters, and an ensuing order from the KMT War Council announcing the disbandment and division of the Fourth Army between the Chinese Communist Party and the KMT, provoked the outbreak of undeclared war which, while helping the Japanese to increase the territory under their occupation, did not arrest the growth of the CCP's influence and the spread of anti-Japanese support bases under its control. The Fourth Army was reinstated and strengthened.

The German invasion of the Soviet Union, and the Red Army's failures during the first phase of the war, resulted in a reduction of immediate Soviet military aid to China, but in global terms the two countries remained allies. The war in China was one of the factors restraining the Japanese from invading the Soviet Union, while the concentration of the large and well-armed Guangdong Army on the Soviet frontier made the war on other fronts more difficult for Japan.

Relations between the central committee of the CCP and the Soviet leaders in the years 1941 to 1945 were far from untroubled. Serving as Comintern's liaison with the CCP, and also as Tass war correspondent in the Special Zone, was P. P. Vladimirov. His diaries, published many years after his death, bear such blatant signs of 'editing', however, that they cannot be taken as a reliable source, but nor can they be totally disregarded.[7] Works published before 1960 in the Soviet Union and China do not deal with the differences between the CCP and the CPSU at all, while in later works they are undoubtedly greatly exaggerated.

The history of the Second World War is sufficiently well known. The USSR and Japan were not formally in a state of war at the beginning of 1945, nor was the outlook very clear. The United States did not yet have the atomic bomb and it was in general still hard to predict whether such a weapon was feasible. England and the USA were afraid that after the total defeat of Germany, which was imminent, they would be dragged into an exhausting war in the Far East and this somewhat inhibited them from taking a sufficiently active part in the solution of Europe's problems. Therefore, at the Yalta Conference of February 1945, a secret agreement was reached on the entry of the USSR into the war against Japan three months after the defeat of Germany.

Only a few months later, however, the situation had changed. The atomic bomb had been made, and American troops had scored impressive victories over the Japanese fleet. The United States and Great Britain, apprehensive of the growth of Soviet influence in the Far East, were now no longer enthusiastic about the Soviet Union's participation in the war with Japan. The Soviet Union, however, had already completed its preparations, and on 8 August 1945 the Soviet government announced that from the next day it would consider itself in a state of war with Japan.

The movement of Soviet troops in Manchuria was swift and after only a few days the main force of the Guangdong army had been destroyed. On 14 August 1945 the Soviet Union and the Chinese republic signed a treaty of friendship and alliance, although the KMT government was in no position to fulfil many of its provisions.

As early as the end of April 1945, the CCP had under its

control territory amounting to almost one million square kilo-metres with a population of some 95 million. The People's Army had more than 900,000 men under arms, while the People's Militia amounted to a further 2,200,000, and self-defence units accounted for up to another 10 million men. By the middle of September, the Peoples' Armies, in an offensive launched by Zhu De on only 10 August, had liberated 315 square kilometres of territory with a population of 20 million.[8] Japan's uncon-ditional surrender was not especially welcome to the KMT, as in many regions of China its armies were in no condition to receive the capitulation of Japanese troops. In many large cities the Japanese garrisons handed their arms over to the People's Liberation Army. In the Manchurian territories liberated by the Soviet Army, a new Chinese administration was created in which organizations of the CCP had overwhelming influence. The Soviet Union did not think the advance into Manchuria of units of the Eighth and Fourth Armies was advisable. However, in Manchurian territory under the control of the CCP, a United Democratic Army began forming and the weapons which Soviet troops had seized as booty from the Guangdong army were handed over to it.

At the beginning of 1946, the Soviet Union was obliged under the terms of its treaty with the Chinese Republic to withdraw its troops from Manchuria. Only a few large cities passed under the control of the KMT as a result, however, and the Chinese Communist Party retained control over most of the regions of Manchuria, Inner Mongolia and north-eastern China. It was pre-cisely this part of the country that became the main political, economic and territorial base for the development of the Chinese revolution, although CCP bases in other regions of China were also strengthened. Speaking at the Eighth Congress of the Chinese Communist Party, the Defence Minister of the Chinese People's Republic, Peng Dehuai, said that in September 1945 the armies of the CCP numbered 1.3 million fighters, and the population of the anti-Japanese bases amounted to 160 million men, creating, in his words, 'a mighty revolutionary force such as had never been seen in the history of the Chinese people.'[9]

Stalin and Mao Zedong: the Soviet Union
and Communist China, 1946–50

Throughout the entire period from 1935 to 1945, Mao Zedong headed the Central Committee of the Chinese Communist Party, and all fundamental political and military directives issued from him. While the majority of Communists accepted Mao's leadership, he had his opponents and enemies in the party, one of whom was Wang Ming who returned to China having been the CCP's representative in Comintern. The factional struggle that went on in the party leadership, albeit in covert form, did not have the effect of weakening Mao's position; on the contrary, it made it all the more solid. The biggest ideological campaign conducted in the CCP in the early 1940s was that organized by Mao 'for an orderly style of work'. Under the slogans of struggling against dogmatism, subjectivism, sectarianism, and 'foreign stereotyped schemes', Mao managed to break the last serious vestiges of opposition to his leadership.

It should be noted, however, that the group led by Mao was the only one capable at that time of conducting an effective struggle in China against the KMT and the Japanese. For that reason he was supported by other leaders who differed from him in many ways, for example Zhou Enlai, Peng Dehuai, Liu Shaoqi, and later on Gao Gang, each one of whom had his own political base. The elements of nationalism in Mao's politics worked only in his favour during the time of the war for national liberation. Had not Stalin also exploited nationalist slogans during the prolonged and bitter war with Germany and the short war with Japan? China had been so utterly oppressed for over a hundred years that nationalism had become a great transforming force which it would have been absurd to ignore. Mao Zedong was being entirely sincere when he told American journalist Emmy Siao:

> The Chinese people are not a flock of obedient sheep. They are a great people with a rich history, a noble national awareness and a lofty understanding of human justice. In the name of national self-respect, human justice and the desire to live on their own land, the Chinese people will never allow the Japanese fascists to turn them into slaves.[10]

It was precisely Communism or Marxism in national colours that led to the formation in China in the mid-1940s of a group of political and military leaders of great stature and experience, the like of which no other Communist party of the time could boast. Naturally, during the anti-Japanese war the Chinese generals deferred to the Soviet generals in their knowledge of modern military technology and the tactics of modern warfare, but they were simultaneously the political leaders of vast regions, whereas Stalin made sure his generals were kept away as far as possible from the political decision-making process. Mao's activities during that time in general helped the CCP to spread its influence in China, and nobody in 1945 could seriously have challenged his ruling position in the party Central Committee.

The Soviet press in the 1970s reproached Mao Zedong and his entourage for having attempted to make contact with the United States at the beginning of the 1940s. But what was criminal in that? America was engaged in a difficult war with Japan, and the main stream of American aid was going to the KMT government. It was perfectly understandable in these circumstances, therefore, to draw America's attention to the possibilities facing the armed forces of the CCP and their need for arms and ammunition. And, in any case, it was precisely at that time that the Soviet Union regarded the United States as an ally in the war against fascism and was not only enjoying substantial economic, military and technical aid from America, but was even insisting that it be increased. The Soviet Union was unable at that time to give the armies of the CCP even the modest degree of help it had given to the liberated regions of China before 22 June 1941, and hence P. P. Vladimirov's complaint that the leaders of the CCP did not give due attention to the small group of Soviet representatives in Yenan rings false and unconvincing.

The situation changed decisively in 1945, when the Soviet Union entered the war against Japan and gave enormous support and aid to the CCP and its armed forces, whereas the United States adopted the course of one-sided and unequivocal help for the KMT. Before the end of the war with Japan, the Seventh Congress of the CCP was convened in the Special Zone in order to set out the contours of the party's political line for the near future, to adopt a new party Statute and complete the formation of the new party leadership. The political report was given by Mao Zedong. Even its title – 'On the coalition government' – was an indication that, having just got rid of the Japanese occupiers, the party was proposing to avoid a civil war and to create a newly democratic society on the basis of a coalition with the KMT. This did not mean, however, that the CCP was prepared to relinquish control over the regions it had liberated, nor to abandon its military formations. The KMT was offered a compromise based on the enhanced role of the CCP and a proposal to introduce anti-feudal and national reforms in the country. In other words, the KMT was offered the chance to participate in the completion of the bourgeois-democratic and national revolution. The KMT of Jiang Gai-shi, however, had long ceased to be a revolutionary party.

The Congress report on the strategic advance against the Japanese was given by Zhu De, while Liu Shaoqi reported on the new party Statute. It was Liu Shaoqi who proclaimed Mao Zedong as 'the leader whom the party had found'. Mao's ideas, which 'united Marxism-Leninism with the experience of the Chinese revolution', were declared to be the ideological basis of the Chinese Communist Party. The cult of Mao, who was now to be called nothing less than the 'great leader of the Chinese revolution', became the political guideline and daily practice for the CCP in the belief that it would consolidate its strength and unity. Today nobody would dispute the harm that the cult of Mao did to both the Chinese Communist Party and the Chinese people. Nor is it disputable that in this the Chinese leaders used as a model the example of the Soviet Union. It was the time when all the large Communist parties emulated the CPSU and found their 'great leader', and the bigger the party or country, the greater or more of a 'genius' its leader.

The period comprising late 1945 and the greater part of 1946 was a time of complex political manoeuvring, with talks between the leaders of the CCP and the KMT, isolated armed confrontations, and preparations for a major civil war. The KMT reinforced its army, which now included troops which the Japanese had organized into puppet formations. The United States supplied Jiang Gai-shi with weapons, ammunition and aircraft, and also sent a number of strong military units, not to speak of countless military advisers and specialists. By the middle of 1946 the KMT had a threefold superiority over the CCP in the terms of regular army numbers.

On the other hand, the CCP was strengthening its own army, as well as its hold over the liberated areas. The Soviet Union withdrew its armies from Manchuria and handed over to the CCP not only a large part of the weaponry it had captured from the Japanese, but also a substantial amount of arms and ammunition taken from Soviet regiments and divisions. A group of Soviet representatives was set up in Manchuria with the task of implementing operational directives in collaboration with the North-Eastern Bureau of the Central Committee of the CCP. The Soviet Union helped with the reconstruction of many factories, highways and bridges; a steady stream of such essential goods as fuel, motor vehicles, cotton fabric, footwear, sugar, salt, medicines and so on flowed from the Soviet Union into Manchuria; Chinese military cadres were given training. To reinforce the rear, the Central Committee decided to resume agrarian reform in the liberated areas. Even though the regular army numbered about 1.5 million men, people's militia units were formed in the liberated areas amounting to more than 3 million men, and self-defence units accounted for a further 10 million.

In the autumn of 1946, the armies of Jiang Gai-shi began a general offensive against the Communist areas of China. In fierce battles the KMT army achieved a number of tactical successes, but it suffered heavy losses, became weary and was weakened by the fighting, and by the spring of 1947 the offensive had been halted. During the previous months the CCP had strengthened its rear and increased the number of its regular troops to 2 million men. Soon the Communists went over to a partial offensive and restored their control over the areas they had previously lost, including many of the large cities of the north-east. Whereas the CCP's control was very firm, the KMT government was incapable of creating a sound power structure in the rest of China, despite the considerable financial, political and military aid it was receiving from the United States.

The Chinese Communists' successes aroused unease in both Washington and Moscow. The Cold War was at its height and it was precisely through that lens that both Truman and Stalin viewed events in China. A 'two Chinas' situation suited Stalin perfectly, as did the analogous 'two Germanys' and 'two Koreas'. Stalin made it very clear that he wanted the CCP to try to obtain from the Kuomintang an arrangement that would somehow preserve a *modus vivendi*, that is to say a compromise by which Jiang Gai-shi's government would retain control of the southern, south-western and central provinces, while the Communists would be able to create their own 'People's Democratic' state in the northern and north-eastern territories where they were in control. This had essentially been Stalin's purpose even as early as the end of 1945, and pressure on the Chinese Communist leaders with that end in view was exerted throughout 1946 and 1947.

Stalin hinted at the desirability of a 'common Far East policy' with the United States during a meeting with the son of the late President Roosevelt. It was glaringly obvious in 1946–7 that neither the Soviet press nor that of the Western Communist parties was giving any information on what was happening in China. The Soviet newspaper reader learned virtually nothing of the large-scale battles between the KMT and Communist armies, nor of the revolutionary transformations going on in north-eastern China. Stalin was convinced that if the Communist offensive developed with further successes, the United States would openly intervene on a massive scale. American intervention would lead to the defeat of the Communists and the occupation of the whole of China by the United States: what Japan had failed to achieve, the United States would achieve with the help of Jiang Gai-shi. China would thus become a vassal of the United States which would hence be able to create its military bases not only in Europe and Japan, but even on the Sino-Soviet border. Stalin voiced these fears in his correspondence with the Chinese leadership.

But he had other still weightier feelings of disquiet, no doubt, about which he said nothing to anybody. He feared the emergence of a Communist state that was more powerful than the USSR and that would be independent of both the USSR and Stalin in its conduct of policy. He knew perfectly well that the Central Committee of the CCP had long been running its own policies and that it had not paid particular attention to Moscow's counsels. Stalin was already having some difficulties with the Communist leaders of Europe, a fact that had led to the creation of Cominform. The choice of Belgrade as the first location of this Communist 'Information Bureau', and of its editorial offices, was no accident. Chinese Communists had not been invited, even as observers, to the meeting in Poland where the decision to create Cominform had been taken.

In this way Stalin facilitated neither a victory for Jiang Gai-shi nor a complete victory for the CCP, since the strengthening of the Chinese Communist Party that would result could undermine the dominating position of the USSR and of Stalin personally in the world Communist movement. The spectre of eastern Titoism seemed to Stalin a greater threat than the Titoism of a relatively small Balkan country. Indeed, while the presence of Russians in Manchuria suited the Chinese Communists, Stalin would admit in 1948 that, after the war, he had advised the 'Chinese comrades' to desist from an actual attempt to come to power.[11]

The leaders of the CCP did not accept Stalin's advice on that occasion. In the latter half of 1947, the People's Liberation Army launched an offensive on a national scale. Led by Deng Xiaoping, Lin Biao, Liu Bocheng and other generals, the CCP armies began their successful drive south, putting pressure on Huai Hai and capturing several of the country's largest cities.

Events unfolded faster than even Mao Zedong had expected. He had reckoned that the war against the KMT would be a long-drawn-out affair, lasting at least five years; yet as early as the second half of 1948 the fundamental breakthrough in the civil war in China had been accomplished, and the main forces of the KMT had been wiped out in a series of systematically executed major military operations. One after another, the country's largest cities came under CCP control: Jinan, Jinru, Zhangzhu, Shenyang, the whole of the north-east and the central valley were liberated from the KMT. In January 1949 Tianjin and Peking were taken. The KMT was still hoping to consolidate its hold in the vast provinces of south-western China, but its hopes there were also dashed. After a short breathing-space, the armies of the CCP renewed their offensive which was now unstoppable. On 24 April 1949, Communist forces captured Nanjing, seat of the KMT government for some time. In May they took Wuhan, Nanchang, and Shanghai. In June all sources of KMT resistance north of the Yangtzijiang (Yangtze) were destroyed. In July and August the main cities and provinces of central-southern, south-eastern and south-western China came under CCP control. By the end of September practically the entire territory of continental China had been freed of KMT troops and only individual, isolated groups continued to show resistance, lasting up to the middle of 1950.

On 1 October 1949 at a solemn ceremony in Peking, the Chinese People's Republic was proclaimed. Mao Zedong was appointed Chairman of the Central People's Government. The revolution had won, even though the liberation of a number of isolated provinces in the south would take a few months more.

The first state officially to recognize the Chinese People's Republic was the Soviet Union, in a declaration published on 2 October, announcing the establishment of diplomatic relations with the new China. No personal letter to Mao Zedong to this effect came from Stalin, however, whose silence was all the more unusual in that only ten days later, on the occasion of the proclamation of the German Democratic Republic, he would send a long personal letter to the first President of the GDR, Wilhelm Pieck, and to the Prime Minister, Otto Grotewohl.

In October and November of 1949, the formation of the Chinese central state institutions took place relatively quickly, in particular the State administrative council, and by the beginning of December, the central government apparatus had virtually been brought up to full strength.

In mid-December 1949, Mao Zedong left China for the first time, heading a large and imposing Chinese delegation to the Soviet Union where, in the company of leaders of other Communist parties, he took part in the celebration of Stalin's 70th birthday. Talks followed, talks which turned out to be long and difficult.

Stalin had few meetings with Mao, and he declined to satisfy many of the requests made by the Chinese government, which was now made to appear in the humiliating role of petitioner. Moreover, difficulties also arose from the fact that Stalin had only recently suffered from a long and serious illness and was making a painful recovery. Finally, the Soviet Union's capacity to help was not yet very great.

Mao and his delegation greeted the New Year in Moscow, but it was not until the middle of February 1950 that a treaty of friendship, union and mutual assistance, to last for 30 years, was signed between the USSR and the Chinese People's Republic. At the same time, an agreement was concluded on the Chinese

Changchun railway, Port Arthur and Dalnii, under which the Soviet Union would retain its naval bases in Port Arthur (Lushun) and Luda (Dalian or Dairen) on the pretext of deterring possible new aggression from Japan.

Before departing, Mao Zedong gave a farewell address at the Yaroslav station in Moscow, in which he said: 'People can see that the unity of two great nations, China and the Soviet Union, reinforced by the treaty, will be eternal, indestructible, and that nobody will ever be able to tear us apart.'[12]

The formation of the Chinese People's Republic was undoubtedly one of the greatest events of the twentieth century. The fact alone of China's unification and the creation of a strong centralized state were of extreme importance. As with Germany and Italy in the nineteenth century, so now the days of a disunited China were past. All three cases came about as the result of historical forces and necessity, but just as Germany's unification without Bismarck, and Italy's without Garibaldi are unthinkable, it is equally hard to imagine China's unification without Mao, although there is no need for us to close our eyes either to his achievements or to his blunders and crimes.

The creation of the Chinese People's Republic changed the geo-political map of the world. Since China declared herself to be the faithful and eternal ally of the Soviet Union, there was no question yet of the formation of a 'strategic triangle'. The West now had to contend not only with the Soviet Union's acquisition of the atomic bomb – it was precisely in 1949–50 that the USSR built and tested its first atomic bombs – but also with the formation of a territorially vast block of allied states stretching from the frontier of West Germany to the South China Sea. Although everybody knew that China was the most populous state in the world, the exact size of the population was not known and was reckoned to be in the region of 450–500 million, but when the first census took place it turned out to be 100 million greater than expected.

The Soviet Union and China: ten years of eternal friendship

China's need for economic and indeed every other kind of aid was somewhat large, while the Soviet Union's capacity was strictly limited. Already, in the period 1946–9, the Soviet Union had done quite a lot to restore the economy of north-eastern China, and now it was said that China was requesting aid to the tune of 3 billion US dollars, but that Stalin would agree to only 300 million, still no mean sum in 1950. Between 1953 and 1960 the Soviet Union undertook responsibility for helping China to build 50 large industrial enterprises, as well as to refurbish and reconstruct the more important branches of its national economy. From the Soviet Union, and soon also from other countries, such as Czechoslovakia and the German Democratic Republic, China began taking delivery of equipment for power stations, metallurgical and mechanical-engineering factories, for coal mines, railway and road transport, and so on. Thousands of young Chinese arrived in the Soviet Union for training in all specialities. It was just at the time I was completing my studies in the Philosophy Faculty at Leningrad University, and in all departments we had Bulgarians, Romanians, Albanians, Czechs and, until 1948 when they had to leave the Soviet Union, Yugo-slavs. Young Chinese men and women probably began to appear in our university hostels in the academic year 1949–50, but unlike the Czechs and Albanians, few of them ever made close friends with Soviet students. Nobody, it seemed, worked as hard as the Chinese students.

The basic job of restoring the national economy, which had been destroyed in the civil war, and of creating the various organs of national government and state administration, was completed in the years 1950 to 1952. Agrarian reform was carried out throughout the whole of China. The country's financial system was stabilized and unemployment was to all intents and purposes eliminated. The widespread banditry which was the usual legacy to be expected from civil war, was wiped out by harsh, swift means. All large-scale enterprises were nationalized, while small private industries were preserved.

At the end of 1952, the chairman of the State Council, Zhou Enlai, declared that the period of restoration had been com-pleted and that the level of the national economy was higher than it had ever been before. Hence, from 1953, they would begin to implement the first Five Year Plan for the construction of China's national economy. This plan had been worked out on the assumption of growing technical, economic and scientific aid from the Soviet Union: 'Learn from the USSR' had been virtually the main slogan in the early 1950s. For example, in one of his speeches at the beginning of 1953 Mao said:

> We intend to bring about a great national reconstruction. The work before us is hard and our experience is inadequate. Therefore we must toil stubbornly, and copy the advanced experience of the Soviet Union. Regardless of whether we are members of the Communist Party, old or young cadre workers, engineers or technologists, intellectuals, workers or peasants, we must all learn from the Soviet Union. . . . In order to build our country, we must bring the job of learning from the Soviet Union up to nation-wide scale.[13]

The Soviet Union and China enjoyed their best relations in the period 1953/4 to 1957/8. For China, it was a time both of rapid economic development and major social and political change. Chief among the social changes was the virtual completion of the collectivization of the peasant and artisan economies and the transformation of the semi-capitalist economy. At the end of 1957 the state sector of the entire Chinese economy amounted to 33 per cent, that of the co-operatives 56 per cent, the state-capitalist part accounted for 8 per cent, and the private individual sector only 3 per cent. Private capitalism had practically disappeared from the economy.[14] Many of these social changes were carried out too hurriedly and gave rise to the illusion that even faster progress was possible. Nevertheless, the overall economic growth was remarkable and corresponded more or less to both the needs and the demands of the country.

In the mid-1950s, China built more than 10,000 industrial enterprises, of which 921 were major enterprises of national significance, 428 of them being fully commissioned and 109 partially so during the Five Year Plan. Each year the growth of industrial production averaged 19.2 per cent, instead of the projected 14.7 per cent, although in absolute terms China's industrial output was still insignificant. Steel output was 5.35 million tonnes, cast iron 5.94 million tonnes, electricity 19.3 billion kilowatts, coal 130 million tonnes, metal-cutting lathes 28,000.[15] In real terms, output of the most important kinds of production in China in 1957 was comparable with Soviet indicators at the end of the first Five Year Plan in 1932. However, the Soviet population at the beginning of the 1930s was only one quarter that of China in 1957. Nevertheless, the results of the first Chinese Five Year Plan must be regarded as a considerable success and an important prerequisite of the country's future development.

Growth in production was not confined to heavy industry. Output of consumer goods went up 89 per cent, railways were extended by 22 per cent to 30,000 kilometres, highways to 250,000 kilometres, air routes to 25,000 kilometres. In five years the number of workers and employees rose from 8 to 24 million.

A tangible increase was also noticeable in the rural economy. The gross yield in food crops increased over the five year period by 22 per cent, and that of cotton by 26 per cent. Livestock numbers rose for pigs, cattle, horses and goats, and technical equipment for farms improved somewhat.[16]

During the first Five Year Plan, China established for herself important economic relations with several capitalist countries, with countries of the Third World and those of East Europe, but by far the greatest help she received in fulfilling the aims of the Five Year Plan in the years 1953–7 came from the Soviet Union.

We mentioned above that Stalin was reserved rather than helpful in promoting the spread of economic aid to China. Yet only two and a half weeks after the death of Stalin, an agreement was signed in Moscow by which the Soviet Union was to help the Chinese People's Republic in the expansion of existing and the construction of new power stations, and two months later another agreement was signed for assistance in the construction and reconstruction of 141 industrial sites, comprising 50 which had come under an agreement of 14 February 1950 and a supplement of 91 large enterprises.[17] The Soviet Union significantly broadened its technical help to China, and a substantial amount of technical documentation was handed over to Chinese enterprises and ministries without charge. By 1953 China's share of the USSR's total external trade turnover amounted to 20 per cent, while the Soviet Union's share of China's total volume of exports was 55.6 per cent.[18]

A Soviet government delegation, consisting of N. S. Khrushchev, N. A. Bulganin and A. I. Mikoyan, attended the fifth anniversary of the founding of the Chinese People's Republic at the end of September 1954. This was the first official visit abroad by the new Soviet leaders. Khrushchev and his colleagues met Mao Zedong several times and they also toured the country widely. Talks between the Soviet and Chinese leaders touched on practically every aspect of relations between the two countries. A large number of agreements were signed in the course of the talks, not all of which were published. The Soviet Union signed an agreement to withdraw its garrison from Port Arthur and to place without cost all military-strategic equipment from the base at the disposal of the Chinese. The Soviet Union gave China its share of the numerous joint stock companies and enterprises, involved in the manufacture of non-ferrous metals, in oil drilling, ship repair and air transport. The decision was taken to commence building railways to China from Ulan-Bator and Alma-Ata. The Soviet Union extended a large new long-term loan, and agreed to increase substantially the number of Soviet specialists working in China, while the number of Chinese undergoing various kinds of training in the Soviet Union was similarly increased. The Soviet Union undertook to increase its deliveries of equipment and to help in the construction of another 15 large-scale projects, and to give considerable aid to the Chinese army in the form of new types of weapons and the training of officers.

These agreements were supplemented over the next four years by a whole host of other agreements: to hand over to China a large quantity of drawings and scientific and technical documentation, to assist in the building of a Chinese experimental nuclear reactor and cyclotron, to exchange exhibitions of each country's achievements in cultural and economic activity, to co-operate in the fields of medicine and sport, education and literature.

In the course of the 1950s, nearly 800 Soviet films were screened in China. A Society for Chinese–Soviet Friendship was formed in China, and one for Soviet–Chinese Friendship came into being in the Soviet Union. When China launched its new Three Red Banners policy in 1958, and its notorious campaign of the Great Leap Forward, the Chinese government requested the acceleration of many deliveries and additions to the list of industrial enterprises being equipped by the Soviet Union. Numerous articles appeared in the Soviet press in the first half of 1958 praising the Great Leap Forward and the People's Communes, but by the latter half of the year it was virtually impossible to find such material any more. Alarming news from China began arriving in

Moscow by various routes, and the whole Three Red Banners policy was arousing considerable concern. Nevertheless, the Soviet Union set out to fulfil the majority of China's requests and greatly increased its aid in 1958 and 1959.

Considering the state and possibilities of the Soviet economy in the 1950s, the scope of Soviet aid to China was very considerable. More than 250 major industrial enterprises, workshops and sites were constructed with Soviet co-operation and equipped with the best Soviet machinery: for example, the Anshan and Wuhan metallurgical complexes, the Changchun automobile factory, the Luoyang factories making tractors, ball-bearings and mining equipment, the Harbin factories making electric motors, turbines and boilers, the Lanzhou oil refinery and synthetic rubber works, the nitrate fertilizer plants at Jilin and Taierzhuang, the slate works at Fujian, the heavy-machinery plant at Fulaerzi, several large power stations and a number of munitions factories, which even today constitute an important part of Chinese industry.

With Soviet help China acquired whole branches of industry that had never existed there before: aviation, automobile and tractor-building, radio and many branches of chemical production. Greatly enhanced capacity was introduced into those industries which had existed on a different technological basis. In overall terms, Chinese production in 1960 from enterprises built with Soviet technical assistance accounted for 35 per cent of cast iron, 40 per cent of steel, more than 50 per cent of rolled iron, 80 per cent of trucks, more than 90 per cent of tractors, 30 per cent of synthetic ammonia, 25 per cent of generated electricity, 55 per cent of steam and hydraulic turbines, about 20 per cent of generators, 25 per cent of aluminium, more than 10 per cent of heavy machinery, and so on.[19]

In the period 1950–60 more than 8,500 technical specialists and 1,500 specialists in science, higher education, health care and culture were sent for varying periods from the Soviet Union to China. The study of Chinese and the training of thousands of translators and interpreters were greatly expanded in the Soviet Union, while in China the study of Russian was even more widely taught. A large number of Soviet military experts worked in China, and at different times more than 1,000 Soviet teachers went there to lecture in the newly created institutes of higher learning. On the other hand, in the 1950s the Soviet Union received about 2,000 Chinese specialists and 1,000 scientists to acquaint them with the experience and achievements of Soviet science and technology.

With the aid of Soviet documentation, 160 sites were planned in China and more than 300 kinds of goods were produced. Joint scientific research projects on 124 subjects were carried out. More than 8,000 Chinese workers, employees and engineers went through production and technical training in Soviet factories in the 1950s, and 11,000 Chinese students and graduates went through Soviet institutes of higher learning and polytechnics. Nearly 900 Chinese scientists worked in the Soviet Academy of Sciences system. China published Soviet literature of all kinds in vast quantities. Chinese economists acknowledged that merely from the free use of the Soviet technical documentation that they had acquired, their country had saved itself several billion dollars. In practice, the Soviet Union and some of the East European countries were China's only source of modern production methods in the 1950s.

Against such a background of active and varied co-operation, isolated disagreements between the two countries went unnoticed. Already in the early 1950s the Soviet press began discussing the question of the so-called 'unequal treaties' in a different way from hitherto. All references to the Address of the Government of the RSFSR to China of 25 May 1919 vanished.[20] The Soviet leaders were clearly dissatisfied with some of the independent actions and decisions which China was taking in its relations with Asian countries and which had not been agreed with Moscow. On the other hand, the Soviet Union did not see any need to consult the Chinese over major acts of its own foreign policy: for example, the sudden *rapprochement* with Yugoslavia, which few expected, or the first attempts at closer relations with the West. The vast campaigns which the Chinese conducted in 1956–7 – building irrigation canals everywhere, the extermination of flies and mosquitoes – and which developed into the policy of the Three Red Banners, were purely Chinese inventions, and Soviet specialists were always critical of such initiatives. On the other hand, the Soviet Union at that time also indulged in adventuristic campaigns, attempting for example to catch up and overtake the United

States in the per capita production of meat, milk and butter. As early as 1954–5 the build-up began of the extremely complex process of Sino-Soviet ideological differences which would become more pronounced after the Twentieth Congress of the CPSU.

As is well known, the world Communist movement in the period from the 1920s to the 1940s was based on hierarchical principles, and although Comintern had been disbanded in 1943, it was still considered that strict unity of views on all basic issues should be adhered to, and that the movement should have a leader. This leader should be not merely one particular party, but one particular man, the most authoritative leader, or, still better, a Marxist–Leninist 'classic'. Up to 1953 there was no doubting that the CPSU was the leader of the world Communist movement, and that the universally recognized Marxist-Leninist 'classic' was obviously Stalin. After his death, however, the situation changed. The CPSU still presented itself as the most authoritative Communist party in the world, if only because it stood at the head of the most powerful socialist state; as for personal leadership, many Chinese believed that the Marx–Engels–Lenin–Stalin line could be continued by only one man, and that was Mao Zedong. In the opinion of many Chinese government people – and pre-eminent among them was Mao himself – not one of the new Soviet leaders could compare with Mao, either in terms of their services to the world Communist movement, or their theoretical contributions to the development of contemporary Marxism. These claims were not made openly, but the fact that the new Soviet leadership dealt with Mao much as they did with the leaders of other large Communist parties and governments of other socialist states, deeply offended Mao's self-esteem.

The Twentieth Congress of the CPSU did more than debunk the cult of Stalin – it also dealt a blow at the cults of other Communist leaders, including Mao Zedong, and this had to be taken into account in China as the materials of the Twentieth Congress became known among the most active members of the CCP. The Chinese press sharply curtailed its eulogies of Mao. The Eighth Congress of the CCP in Peking changed the formulation of the party's ideological foundations, passed at the Seventh Congress, and deleted the phrase: 'The Chinese Communist

Party is guided in all its actions by the thoughts of Mao Zedong, uniting as they do the theory of Marxism–Leninism with the experience of the Chinese revolution.'[21]

Deng Xiaoping devoted his Congress report to the principles of collective leadership and the broadening of internal party democracy, and said:

> Of course, the cult of personality is a social phenomenon with a long history and it could not but find its reflection to some degree in our party and social life. Our task is decisively to continue to carry out the policy of the Central Committee which is directed against over-emphasis on the personality and its glorification; our task is genuinely to strengthen the ties between the leaders and the masses, in order that in all spheres the line of the masses and the democratic principles of the party are carried out.[22]

The Twentieth Congress of the CPSU put forward a number of propositions which ran counter to the views of Mao Zedong, for example on the need to avert a new world war. Although the Chinese press formally upheld the line taken at the Twentieth Congress, on the unofficial level Mao Zedong criticized several of the Congress's propositions. The *People's Daily*, an organ over which Mao himself exercised ultimate editorial control, published barely masked criticism of Khrushchev's secret speech in the form of articles entitled 'On the historical experience of the dictatorship of the proletariat' and 'Once more on the historical experience of the dictatorship of the proletariat'; these were reprinted in *Pravda*.

A more moderate and ambiguous point of view expressed in Peking found its adherents in Moscow, where rumours were circulating about Chinese dissatisfaction with Khrushchev's 'high-risk' policies, and also about unofficial or even secret contacts between the Chinese leadership and Khrushchev's opponents in the Communist Party Central Committee. At any rate, it is clear that it was certainty of firm support from Peking that prompted Molotov, Malenkov, Kaganovich and their supporters to come out against Khrushchev in June 1957. The result of the June 1957 Plenum of the Party Central Committee, however, was a victory for Khrushchev and the consolidation of his position in the Party leadership. Mao Zedong would of course have been delighted had the Molotov group won the day, but he had nevertheless to accept the facts of the situation.

The Chinese leaders followed events in Eastern Europe and the Middle East closely, and all the main measures adopted by the Soviet Union in these areas were taken in consultation with China. However, both the Soviet Union and China dealt with many problems, domestic and foreign, totally independently of each other and without prior consultation. Almost nobody in the Soviet Union could understand the political campaigns of 1956–7, such as the struggle against the 'rightist' elements and the movement that went under the slogan 'let a hundred flowers blossom, let all scientists compete'.

Mao Zedong visited the Soviet Union for the second time in 1957 with a group of other Chinese leaders in order to take part in the 40th anniversary celebrations of the October Revolution. It is known that, following the celebrations, a conference of leaders from socialist countries took place, as well as an international conference of Communist parties. The reports of these conferences have never been published, but in short communiqués it was stated, in particular, that the participants had approved the decisions of the Twentieth Party Congress, as well as the foreign and domestic policies of the USSR. Criticism was aimed chiefly at Yugoslavia, which had not attended the Moscow meetings.

While Mao did not enter into open polemics with the Soviet speakers, his speeches were, however, different from those of many other Communist leaders. This even concerned the question of the possibility of another world war. The line taken by the Twentieth Congress had been that, if a new world war were nevertheless to be unleashed, it would be neither the whole world nor mankind, but imperialism that would perish. The Soviet press did not elaborate further on this formulation, but Mao was in general agreement with the Congress's new line and in his conversations and speeches he frequently elucidated his understanding of this particular thesis. His pronouncements on the subject were not just utterly frank, they seemed to his interlocutors at times even cynical, though it would be several years before the polemics began over many of his formulations. Some of Mao's utterances were not reproduced in the Soviet press until

1963. According to one source, Mao said at the Moscow conference of Communist parties:

> Can one guess at the number of human casualties a future war would cause? It might be one third of the entire 2,700 million of the world's population, that is, 900 million. I think that figure is too small, if atomic bombs really are going to be used. That is terrible, of course, but it would not be so bad if even half were killed. Why? Because it was not we who wanted the war, but they, they, who thrust it on us. If we fight, then atomic and hydrogen bombs will be used. I personally think that there would be such suffering in the whole world that half the world's population would perish, maybe more than half. I argued about this with Nehru. He was more pessimistic about this than I am. I told him that if half the world's population was destroyed, then the other half would be left, but then imperialism would have been utterly destroyed and throughout the world there would only be socialism, and in 50 or 100 years the population would increase, perhaps by more than half again.[23]

While both the CPSU and the CCP kept polemics out of their public speeches, the mutual criticism voiced at closed sessions mounted steadily. As early as January 1957 at a party meeting Mao Zedong – borrowing a quotation from Stalin – said that Khrushchev was obviously 'dizzy with success'. Mao was criticizing Soviet agricultural policy and defending Chinese domestic policy under the slogan 'let a hundred flowers blossom'. Some aspects of Soviet foreign policy were also subjected to criticism, but at the same time many facets of both Chinese domestic and foreign policy were being criticized at closed sessions in the Soviet Union. With some cause, the Soviet leadership doubted whether the Three Red Banners, the Great Leap Forward, the Liquidation of the Four Evils, and a number of other campaigns were correct courses for the Chinese to take. Both parties, let it be said, gave grounds for criticism at that time: both Khrushchev and Mao Zedong committed a number of errors of various kinds at the end of the 1950s.

Just when the Soviet Union was making efforts to improve relations with the United States, China was firing shells at Jiang Gai-shi's troops on the islands in the Straits of Formosa, thus putting great strain on US–Chinese relations. Differences arose between China and the Soviet Union in 1957–8 over military co-operation. The Soviet Union was evidently not keen to supply the Chinese with the technology and technical aid which they needed in order to create their own atomic and hydrogen bombs and rockets. On the other hand, China declined the Soviet pro-posal to build a special radio station on Chinese territory and also refused the Soviet request that Soviet naval vessels be allowed to enter Chinese ports. The Soviet Union for its part refused the Chinese request for a Soviet-built fleet of nuclear-powered submarines, which annoyed and offended Mao Zedong. To try to iron out these differences, Khrushchev decided to make a secret and unofficial visit to China, where he spent four days, 31 July to 3 August, 1958, meeting Mao every day. Their fundamental disagreements, however, remained un-resolved.

A new spate of disagreements between the CPSU and the CCP erupted in the summer and autumn of 1959. The Chinese leaders did not hide their displeasure at Khrushchev's hurried trip to the USA and the prospect of improved Soviet–US relations, and when Khrushchev, soon after his return from Washington, flew to Peking for the tenth anniversary of the Chinese People's Republic, he found a very cold reception waiting for him. Mao Zedong and Liu Shaoqi were at the airport for a polite meeting, but their motorcade drove through empty streets. Mao Zedong, moreover, pleading a heavy workload, avoided long and serious discussion. It was hardly surprising, therefore, that as soon as the official ceremonies were done with, Khrushchev quit China. That was the last time a Soviet leader visited Peking. In the 25 years that have elapsed since that trip, not one summit meeting has been organized between the two countries.

The Soviet Union and China diverged further and further over questions of foreign policy. During the armed border conflict between China and India, the Soviet Union took a neutral posi-tion, sympathizing if anything with India rather than China. The differences between the two countries soon began to touch on a whole range of questions involving the national liberation move-ments in Asia, Africa and Latin America.

Economic relations between the Soviet Union and China also worsened. During China's first Five Year Plan, the USSR had been China's chief trading partner, but in 1959 the volume of

Sino-Soviet trade began to decline sharply. This was due in part to the collapse of the Great Leap Forward, but also to the deterioration of their political relations. Mutual criticism became more and more open; in the Soviet Union one could hear it in the tone of the propaganda, whereas in China it was carried out far more openly. At the same time an exchange of private letters took place. In the spring of 1960 the Soviet government invited Mao Zedong to come to the USSR for a rest and talks, but Mao declined the invitation. Gradually, the disagreements between the USSR and China became the object of discussion in other Communist parties when, in June 1960, the Central Committee of the CPSU sent a special 'Information Notice' to all Communist parties, containing criticism of the doctrinal views of the Chinese Communist leaders and their claims against the USSR. The Chinese leadership similarly sent a special letter to the leading organs of other Communist parties.

Then the Chinese began distributing some of the documents containing their criticisms of the USSR among the Soviet specialists working in China. After several protests, which the Chinese ignored, Khrushchev took a sudden and plainly mistaken decision. On 16 July 1960, the Chinese Ministry of Foreign Affairs was handed a note stating that the Soviet Union was recalling all its specialists. As later events would show, this was a decision that would have had to be taken sooner or later, but in the summer of 1960 it was hasty and politically ill thought out, an example of Khrushchev's impulsive actions that were to become more and more frequent, dictated not so much by sober reasoning as by irritation and impatience.

Just at that moment, China was going through particularly serious economic difficulties, brought about by the collapse of the Three Red Banners campaign; the recall of the Soviet specialists could only deepen and complicate her problems. Khrushchev's step cast doubt on the Soviet assertion that Soviet economic aid to the less developed countries was not bound up with political conditions. The Chinese, moreover, could now claim that many of their problems were precisely connected with the sudden cessation of Soviet economic and technical aid, although that was, of course, an obvious exaggeration. There were in all only 1,600 Soviet specialists working in China in 1960, not a large number for such a large country. However, one should not underestimate the scale of the damage to China, which for a while had to abandon several important projects; and the withdrawal of the specialists was accompanied by a considerable reduction of all other kinds of economic and technical aid.

The recall of the Soviet specialists did not yet signal the complete breakdown of relations between the two countries. Preparations began in the middle of the year for the new International Conference of Communist parties, in which all the Communist parties of the world, except Yugoslavia, would take part. The minutes have never been published, but it is known that the differences between the USSR and China were one of the most important items on the conference agenda. Practically every one of the 81 parties attending the conference in Moscow took the side of the CPSU. The Chinese delegation, headed by Liu Shaoqi, defended its position for many days, but they were isolated and, following the instructions of the Central Committee of the CCP, they signed the closing declaration of the conference.

At the Soviet government's invitation, Liu Shaoqi did not leave Moscow at once, but toured the country and had meetings with Khrushchev, who several times expressed the wish to open a new phase in the development of inter-state and inter-party relations. At first it looked as if this approach might be successful. The *People's Daily* wrote at the time: 'The current visit of President Liu Shaoqi has undoubtedly strengthened and developed still further the great friendship and bond of the peoples of China and the Soviet Union and it has written a golden page into the history of Soviet–Chinese friendship.'[24]

The same words were repeated in Mao's New Year greetings telegrams to Khrushchev and Brezhnev in 1961. But they were only words. The era of the 'great friendship and the bond between the Chinese and Soviet peoples' had come to an end.

The Soviet Union and China: 20 years of hostility

The compromise reached at the end of 1960 between the Soviet Union and China proved to be both unstable and short-lived. China's economic position deteriorated rapidly and this generated a sharp political struggle within the Chinese leadership. Mao Zedong managed to gain the upper hand over a group led by the Defence Minister, Peng Dehuai, which had severely criticized the Three Red Banners policy. Peng Dehuai was removed from office and placed under house arrest, his post now being occupied by Lin Biao who promptly launched a campaign 'to turn the army into a school for the thoughts of Mao Zedong'. In a matter of three months, from July 1960 to February 1961, he dismissed more than 3,000 defence staff. On the other hand, Mao was forced to step down from his post as Chairman of the Chinese People's Republic and to hand it over to Liu Shaoqi, whose supporters had been endeavouring to change, even if only partially, the reckless Three Red Banners policy. Mao remained chairman of the CCP, however, and continued to hold the main levers of power in his hands. The country began to experience hunger, the full scale of which was carefully concealed, and only after many years did it become known that in 1960–1 no less than 6 or 7 million people had died of starvation. Under the circumstances, it was prudent of Mao to move out of the limelight for the time being.

A painful policy of 'adjustment' was now proclaimed. Both industrial and agricultural output were reduced by approximately 30 per cent. Annual turnover of trade with the Soviet Union was cut to a third. The Chinese government declined Soviet help in the construction of 124 sites, but requested that co-operation continue on the construction of 66 existing sites. The volume of Soviet deliveries of complete equipment in 1961 shrank to one fifth.[25] At numerous closed meetings and conferences, the Chinese identified Soviet policy as the most important cause of the failures in the Chinese economy.

For its part, Soviet propaganda was also beginning noticeably to change its judgement and tone when the subject was 'our great and powerful eastern ally'; even as early as 1959–60, a stricter censorship was introduced in all publications about China, and all mention of the Great Leap Forward and the People's Communes was forbidden. I was working at that time in a large Soviet publishing house, and it was obvious to me that Chinese subjects were beginning to disappear from the forward plans of all the biggest publishing houses. As an odd example, a group of Soviet women workers from Ivanovo visited China in 1958 and were shown the latest textile factories and the best People's Communes. A book was written on the basis of their impressions and the materials they had collected, but the publishing authorities in their oblast held up its publication. The book did not come out until 1961, and then it drew sharp condemnation in Moscow. The gross error of the Ivanovo publishing authorities, oblast censorship offices and oblast party committee was discussed at a special session of the Central Committee Bureau for the RSFSR. In the 1950s such Chinese journals had appeared in Russian as *People's China* and *Friendship*, as well as occasional pamphlets, embassy leaflets and so on, but now they were all stopped.

Even so, when the Twenty-second Congress of the CPSU opened in Moscow in October 1962, there among the countless guests were the delegation from China, led by Zhou Enlai, whose speech at the Congress nevertheless contained some oblique criticism of CPSU policy. Pleading other commitments, the Chinese premier left Moscow before the end of the Congress. N. S. Khrushchev personally accompanied him to the airport, which indicated that the Soviet Union did not wish to sharpen the polemics. However, at the very next closed meeting of senior Chinese Communists, Zhou Enlai labelled the Twenty-second Congress 'revisionist', took up the defence of the Albanian delegation, which had left the Congress, and once again laid the chief blame for China's present economic difficulties squarely on the shoulders of the Soviet Union.

Suddenly, in 1962, China utterly refused to take delivery of complete equipment that had been ordered from the Soviet Union and Eastern Europe. Over the next two years, the Soviet Union repeatedly offered to send groups of specialists whose help was essential if the difficult economic problems the Chinese were experiencing were to be solved, but the Chinese government requested such help rarely, and even then they only wanted small groups of ten to fifteen. Cultural exchange between the two countries practically came to a standstill. China ceased publishing Soviet scientific and technical literature, or receiving Soviet documentation, or showing Soviet films. The exchange of all kinds of notes and letters containing every sort of accusation and criticism, however, expanded to greater and greater volume. Memoranda composed in Moscow were despatched to Peking, notes written in Peking went back to Moscow – all this correspondence, it should be noted, still of a confidential nature.

The political quarrel between the CCP and the CPSU – viewed

by President Kennedy as 'America's great hope' – became more open and much sharper in 1963. From the beginning of the year, the *People's Daily* and other Chinese organs began printing a series of articles attacking the policies of the Soviet Union and the CPSU; material that was even cruder and more hostile, both in style and content, was reprinted from the Albanian press; articles attacking the Italian, French, American and other Communist parties started appearing.

In the spring of 1963 the Soviet Union made a new effort to end the polemics which were becoming more and more intense. Khrushchev proposed a meeting of Soviet and Chinese leaders, either at the highest or at a 'high' level. The Chinese side responded by agreeing to a meeting at a 'high' level. Evidently not expecting a meeting to take place, however, they published a lengthy paper, outlining their view of the questions at issue and consisting of 25 points, entitled *Proposals on the general line of the international Communist movement*. There is no sense now in analysing that pretentious, scholastic, extremely dogmatic document. It was not published by the Soviet government, which did not wish to complicate the forthcoming meeting with the Chinese delegation, planned for July, but the Chinese embassy and several other Chinese organizations attempted wherever they could to distribute the *Proposals*, which had been translated into Russian for mass circulation as a sort of Chinese 'samizdat'. Chinese radio broadcasts to the Soviet Union throughout this time carried material and information all critical of CPSU policies. They were not jammed, but nobody listened to them anyway.

The meeting between CPSU and CCP representatives, which began on 5 July 1963, took place in an unpromising political atmosphere. The Chinese side was led by Party General Secretary Deng Xiaoping, and the Soviet side by M. A. Suslov. Just as the talks got under way, the Soviet press published all 25 points of the Chinese *Proposals*, as well as an *Open letter from the Central Committee of the CPSU to all party organizations and all Soviet Communists*, containing an all-out criticism of the 'general line' being proposed by the Chinese Communist Party.

In many respects, this extensive document gave a valid response to many of the issues then facing the international Communist movement, but it also contained not a few mistaken